WORLD
CULTURES
in Perspective

East Asian
Cultures
IN PERSPECTIVE

Joanne Mattern

Mitchell Lane
PUBLISHERS
P.O. Box 196
Hockessin, Delaware 19707

Mitchell Lane

PUBLISHERS

Printing   1   2   3   4   5   6   7   8   9

Library of Congress Cataloging-in-Publication Data
Mattern, Joanne, 1963-
 East Asian cultures in perspective / by Joanne Mattern.
      pages cm. — (World cultures in perspective)
 Includes bibliographical references and index.
 ISBN 978-1-61228-564-1 (library bound)
1. East Asia—Civilization—Juvenile literature. 2. East Asia—Social life and customs—Juvenile literature. I. Title.
 DS509.3.M43 2014
 951—dc23

                                        2014019371

eBook ISBN: 9781612286037

PUBLISHER'S NOTE: This story is based on the author's extensive research, which she believes to be accurate. Documentation of this research is on pages 60–61.

The Internet sites referenced herein were active as of the publication date. Due to the fleeting nature of some web sites, we cannot guarantee they will all be active when you are reading this book.

To reflect current usage, we have chosen to use the secular era designations BCE ("before the common era") and CE ("of the common era") instead of the traditional designations BC ("before Christ") and AD (*anno Domini,* "in the year of the Lord").

PBP

CONTENTS

INTRODUCTION

Asia is the largest continent on Earth. It covers about 30 percent of Earth's land area and is home to 4.3 billion people. The continent is filled with differences in climate, landforms, political systems, and ethnic groups.

The huge continent is divided into smaller sections. One of the most important is East Asia, which includes China, Japan, Mongolia, North Korea, South Korea, and Taiwan. Some East Asians are farm dwellers who are at home in simple shelters in the countryside and live much like their grandparents did. Many others live in crowded cities, where they use the latest technology and have access to other cultures worldwide.

Historically, East Asian countries were often cut off from other parts of the world for long periods of time. This isolation allowed nations such as Japan, China, and Korea to develop their own unique cultures. In many ways these cultures were more advanced and elaborate than cultures that developed in Europe and the Americas during the same time. East Asian countries also experienced governments that strictly controlled every aspect of life. Such restrictions kept these nations separate from the rest of the world and allowed them to form very distinct traditions.

During the mid- to late twentieth century, East Asian countries faced dramatic changes in their governments and became more exposed to Western nations. Because of this contact, most East Asian countries (except North Korea) have greatly changed, especially over the past twenty years. As Western influences became popular in these countries, ancient traditions and customs began to disappear. However, these ancient traditions are so important in Asian life that many remain a big part of their cultures today.

In the past, East Asia and its people were a great mystery. Today the nations of East Asia have opened up to the rest of the world. Let's learn more about East Asia!

Shanghai, China

CHAPTER ONE
Gung Hay Fat Choy!

 Gung Hay Fat Choy! Happy New Year! In Western countries, New Year's Day is mostly a holiday for adults, and most of the festivities take place on one night. In East Asian countries, things are very different.

Asians call this holiday the Lunar New Year or Spring Festival. The holiday is called Lunar New Year because the date of the new year is determined by the lunar calendar, which goes by the phases of the moon. Because the Asian calendar follows the moon, New Year's Day falls on a different day each year—but always during January or February.

Lunar New Year is the longest holiday in the Asian calendar— and a busy, happy time in East Asia. While Western countries have just one night to celebrate, a Lunar New Year's celebration lasts for fifteen days. Preparations start well before the holiday. There is so much to do!

First, people have to clean their houses to get rid of clutter and dust. Lunar New Year is also a time for families to get together. This is especially important in today's society because so many relatives move far away from home to find jobs or go to school. Lunar New Year gives them a chance to reunite with their families. China's national news agency, Xinhua, estimated that 3.62 billion journeys would take place during 2014 celebrations. In Korea, 2013 saw 30 million people traveling by bus, car, train, or plane.[1]

Although the Lunar New Year celebrations last for over two weeks, the first night is the most exciting. The fun starts with a big family dinner on New Year's Eve. In northern China, traditional foods are served, such as fish or dumplings. Both of these foods are said to bring prosperity in the new year.[2]

Fireworks explode above the city of Tsuchirura, Ibaragi Prefecture, Japan.

When midnight comes, things get noisy. One member of the family stays up to meet the New Year's monster, a tradition called "Shou Sui."[3] People have to scare the monster away by making a lot of noise. One of the best ways to do this is with firecrackers, so lots of noisy firecrackers are set off all through the New Year's holiday.

Noisy parades are another way to scare off monsters and bring good luck. On New Year's Day, many people gather for a parade. This parade is usually led by the figure of a dragon because dragons are good luck in Asian cultures. Two people also dress up as a lion to perform a special Lion Dance. These celebrations are loud, fun ways for Asians to express their culture and traditions.

One of the most popular New Year's traditions in China is the red envelope. Children are given small red envelopes that contain money as a New Year's gift. The red color and the gift of money are supposed to protect the child who receives it from evil and sickness and bring good luck in the New Year.

Dancers dressed in lion costumes are an important feature of most New Year's parades in China.

If you go to Asia during Lunar New Year, you will see the lucky color red everywhere. People hang red lanterns in their homes and businesses. A Chinese symbol called "Fu" is also hung upside-down on the door of a house. Fu means luck, happiness, and prosperity, and hanging this symbol upside-down shows that these lucky qualities are coming in the New Year.[4]

The Lunar Calendar

The lunar calendar runs on a twelve-year cycle, and each year corresponds to a different animal. Asians believe each animal has specific characteristics, and a person born in that year also has those characteristics. Here is what each animal means:

Rat: Intelligent, charming, quick-witted, sociable.

Ox: Loyal, reliable, strong, determined.

Tiger: Brave, enthusiastic, ambitious, confident.

Rabbit: Trustworthy, sincere, modest, caring.

Dragon: Lucky, imaginative, artistic.

Snake (sometimes called Little Dragon): Organized, intelligent, decisive.

Horse: Loyal, brave, ambitious, intelligent, adventurous.

Sheep: Tasteful, elegant, charming, sensitive, calm.

Monkey: Quick-witted, charming, lucky, smart, lively.

Rooster: Honest, energetic, intelligent, confident.

Dog: Loyal, friendly, brave.

Boar: Honorable, generous, determined, optimistic.[5]

CHAPTER TWO
Chinese Culture

道 China is the third largest country in the world—only Russia and Canada are larger. China is larger than the entire continent of Australia and almost as big as the continent of Europe. This giant nation is home to an ancient and fascinating culture.

History

Modern humans have lived in China for at least 130,000 years. Early natives were nomads who traveled from place to place to find food. Later, people grew crops and raised livestock, which allowed them to live in one place year-round. In time, they settled in small communities and then larger cities.

For centuries China was ruled by royal families called "dynasties." During the Han dynasty, which lasted from 206 BCE until 220 CE, China began trading with other people in central Asia. Merchants established travel routes that became known as the Silk Road because so many people journeyed to China to buy the beautiful silk fabric made there.

Students, merchants, and other travelers came to China during the Tang dynasty, which lasted from 618 to 907. Other dynasties followed, and so did more contact with other cultures. However, China's population grew too large to grow enough food for everyone. It was also difficult for the government to rule so many people living in such an enormous area.

By 1911 Great Britain, Russia, Japan, France, and the United States were involved in China's affairs. This angered many Chinese, who wanted to keep their traditional customs and manage their own country. In 1911 the people rebelled and got rid of the last dynasty. The next year the Republic of China was established, and Dr. Sun Yat-sen became China's first president. After Sun Yat-sen died in 1925, his army commander, Chiang Kai-shek, took power. A long war followed. Finally in 1949 Mao Zedong and the Communist Party won control of China. The Communists believed that the government should own all businesses and completely control the economy. Chairman Mao, as he was called, proclaimed a new nation, the People's Republic of China, on October 1, 1949.

Communism wholly changed China. Aside from taking control of all businesses and industries, the government took land away from farmers. China also cut ties with most of the rest of the world. During Chairman Mao's rule, few people could travel into or out of China.

Chairman Mao died in 1976. Deng Xiaoping became China's next leader in 1978. Deng allowed more freedom and introduced some democratic ideas into Chinese culture and government during his fourteen-year rule. He also opened China's borders to other countries. Finally it was possible for foreigners to visit China.

Sun Yat-sen

China's People and Families

China has the largest population of any country on Earth. More than 1.3 billion people, or about one-fifth of everyone on Earth, live in China. Most Chinese people live in the eastern and southern parts of the country. As you go farther north and west, the population is smaller.

With such a large population, it's no surprise that China has many different ethnic groups—fifty-six in all. The largest ethnic group is the Han Chinese. They make up about 92 percent of China's population.[1] Han Chinese live in most of the urban areas of China as well as in the northeastern, central, and southern parts of the country.

Many of China's other ethnic groups live near the borders with neighboring countries. Many Mongolians and Kazakhs live in the northern part of China, near the borders of Mongolia and Kazakhstan. Western China has a large population of Tibetans. Other ethnic groups include Uighurs, Zhuangs, Dia, Hui, and Li.

Barkhor Square is a lively marketplace and gathering spot for pilgrims, tourists, and locals in Lhasa, Tibet.

In addition, people with Korean and Russian backgrounds also make up China's population.

Family is extremely important to the Chinese people, who believe a strong family is the basis of a good society. In the past, Chinese families were very large. Because most families lived in rural areas, they needed plenty of relatives to farm the land. However, Chinese families have gotten much smaller over the years. Most now have only one or two children, especially if they live in cities.

It is common for several generations of a family to live together. Sons take care of their elderly parents, so a household might include one or two parents, their son and his wife, and one or two grandchildren. Daughters usually end up taking care of their in-laws since they are part of the husband's family.

A Chinese family plants flowers together.

In the past parents chose who their children would marry. Often a matchmaker found a suitable husband or wife. Today most young people are free to choose their spouse. Couples marry either in a traditional ceremony or by a government official in an office. Because red is a lucky color in China, traditional Chinese brides wear red dresses. However, white gowns are increasingly popular as China adopts more Western customs.[2]

Religion

The Communist government does not believe in religion, but traditional religious beliefs are still very important to many Chinese people. Buddhism, the most popular religion in China, follows the teachings of Siddhartha Gautama Buddha, who lived about 2,500 years ago. Buddha had a privileged life, but when he realized many people were suffering, he left home to try to understand the meaning of life and find the way to truth and happiness.[3]

Buddhism teaches people to live in harmony with nature and to perform good deeds. There are many Buddhist temples all over China where people pray and leave gifts for Buddha, such as food. They also honor Buddha by lighting sticks of incense, which makes a sweet, smoky smell. People believe that gifts and incense will make Buddha happy, and he will give them good fortune.

Literature, Music, and Art

China has a rich cultural heritage. Chinese people express their culture through stories, art, theater, and music.

Chinese myths feature many different characters, such as Lei Gong, the god of thunder. These stories also include fantastic animals like the dragon. In China, dragons are symbols of strength and prosperity. Myths and stories later became the themes of poetry and drama.

Chinese art is very beautiful and takes many different forms. Early paintings and sculptures focused on everyday subjects, including animals and people. Later, landscape paintings became popular. Chinese art also features mythological creatures, such as dragons. Sculptors often use precious stones like jade to

Traditional Chinese temple building

Jade
Buddha
statue

create beautiful figures. Chinese people also enjoy folk crafts, such as paper-cutting and embroidery.

Music is very important in Chinese life. Traditional Chinese music does not sound like Western music. Instead it features percussion instruments, including gongs, bells, and drums, along with flutes and pipes and stringed instruments like the *erhu* (a fiddle with two strings) and the *guqin* (a stringed instrument that rests on a table or a person's lap while it is played).

The most traditional form of Chinese music and theater is opera. Chinese opera began more than a thousand years ago.[4] Operas feature elaborate costumes and makeup. Performers don't just sing, they also dance and do acrobatics as they tell stories based on old folktales and legends.

Chinese Culture Today

Life in China has changed tremendously in the past forty years. China was once a mysterious nation cut off from the rest of the world. Life and culture went on behind a curtain of secrecy, and it was easier for the Chinese people to maintain their traditions and beliefs. Things changed when economic reforms took over during the 1980s. Many people left home to find jobs in cities or even went to work overseas. It became harder for Chinese families to stay together. Also, as more people moved to cities, more housing was needed, so traditional Chinese homes and neighborhoods were torn down and replaced by large apartment buildings.

Technology has also changed China. Even though the government strictly controls the country's media and the Internet, Chinese people can find out what's going on in other parts of the world. They now listen to Western-style music and wear Western clothes,

Sichuan Opera
in Chengdu

celebrate some Western holidays, and eat Western foods. Restaurants such as Starbucks, McDonald's, and Pizza Hut are easy to find in China's cities.[5]

Tourism is another reason for the change in Chinese culture. In 2012 nearly fifty-eight million foreign tourists came to China, making it the third-most-visited country in the world.[6] These visitors bring their own customs and beliefs into China, allowing Chinese natives to discover a different way of life.

Despite the rapid changes in China over the past forty years, the basic culture has remained very much the same. China's people still believe in family and peace. They enjoy traditional music and storytelling and pass these tales on to their children and grandchildren. They celebrate traditional holidays and follow ancient customs just as their ancestors did. In some ways Chinese culture is as strong as ever.

Internet cafés, such as this one in Qingdao, China, are popular gathering places for many Chinese citizens.

Gender Roles: Men and Women in China

Many cultures view men as stronger than women, and the Chinese were no different. Men were viewed as powerful providers, while women generally stayed home to care for their husbands and children. This followed an ancient Chinese belief in "yin and yang," which are two forces that are so opposite that they balance each other out (for example, weak and strong). Traditionally, a Chinese woman had to obey three men in her life: her father, her husband, and her son.[7]

When Chairman Mao and the Communist Party came to power, things changed dramatically. Mao viewed women and men as equals and struck down many barriers that had held women back. For the first time, women could work at the same jobs men did and receive the same education as their brothers. Men and women also dressed the same way, which further emphasized equality. Today many Chinese women work outside the home and hold important positions in business and government.

CHAPTER THREE
Mongolian Culture

道 Travel north of China and you will reach the East Asian country of Mongolia. Completely surrounded by the countries of China and Russia, Mongolia has no coastline. The country measures 603,909 square miles, about the size of Alaska. This nation has a rich culture that dates back thousands of years.

History

At one time Mongolia was a vast empire that stretched across more than eleven million square miles. The first important Mongol leader was Genghis Khan. His grandson Khublai Khan became one of the most powerful rulers in the world. By 1260 Khublai Khan had conquered China and ruled a huge empire that stretched from what is now Korea to Hungary and included most of Asia except for today's India.

However, such a huge nation was impossible to rule. Many tribes rebelled, and Khan also faced attacks from groups along the borders. By the time Khublai Khan died in 1294, the Mongol empire was already falling apart.

Over the next four hundred years, Mongolia was torn apart by war. Then in 1691 China took over Mongolia. Beginning in 1911, Mongolia tried to win its freedom from China. But it wasn't until 1921 and with help from Russia that Mongolia was liberated and declared its independence.

By the 1920s Russia had come under Communist rule, and the Communist party took over Mongolia's government as well. Mongolia was soon cut off from the rest of the world. It wasn't until the fall of Communism in 1990 that Mongolia finally elected a democratic government. Slowly, the nation opened up to the rest of the world.

**Statue of
Genghis Khan**

CHAPTER THREE

Mongolia's People and Families

For most of its history, Mongolia was a nation of nomadic herders who raised sheep, cattle, camels, goats, and horses. The country has many grasslands, called steppes, that are perfect for grazing cattle. Mongolian herders traveled with their livestock, moving from place to place depending on the seasons and the availability of food for the animals.

This nomadic, rural lifestyle has had a huge influence on Mongolian life and culture. Having long depended on the land for everything they needed, Mongolian people have a deep love for nature. They have few possessions and readily pack up and move to a new location in search of better food or to escape the country's extreme weather conditions.

However, just like China, people in Mongolia are adopting different lifestyles. Many citizens have given up the harsh, poor existence of the rural life to move into cities. The nation's capital, Ulaanbaatar, grew by about 30,000 people every year between 1999 and 2006.[1] Today about half of Mongolia's people live in

View of Ulaanbaatar

cities, while about one-quarter are year-long nomads. The rest of the population divides their time between a nomadic life on the steppes in the summer and life in villages during the winter.[2]

Because Mongolia has harsh geographic features, including deserts, mountains, and steppes, people must rely on each other to survive, and hospitality is one of Mongolia's most important traditions. Guests are always welcomed and given food such as hot tea, milk, cheese, and sweets. Travelers are invited to sleep in the *gers*, or huts, rural Mongolians call home. In the cities too visitors are always met with hospitality.

Religion

Most people in Mongolia are Buddhist, following teachings from hundreds of years ago. However, during the Communist rule, people were forbidden to practice Buddhism or any other religion. At least 17,000 monks were killed during the 1920s and 1930s, and most monasteries were destroyed.[3] During the Communist era, people practiced Buddhism in secret. This kept Buddhist rituals,

traditions, and holidays alive. After the fall of Communism, people rediscovered their Buddhist faith. New monasteries and schools opened, and the government began restoring temples. Today Buddhism is once again the most common religion in Mongolia.

Sports and Arts

Sports have always been an important part of Mongolian culture. The three most popular sports are horse racing, wrestling, and archery. Horseback riding has been an important skill in Mongolia for centuries and a vital part of the nomadic lifestyle. An old saying acknowledges this: "Mongols are born on horseback."

Like horseback riding, archery is another ancient skill that has become a popular sport. Wrestling is also popular and allows men of all shapes and sizes to test their strength against each other.

As in other East Asian countries, art is important in Mongolian culture. Historically, much of Mongolia's art expressed Buddhist religious beliefs, so traditional arts were forbidden during Communist rule. After the fall of Communism, people returned to age-old forms of expression, including singing and other types of music.

One of the most beautiful arts in Mongolia is the creation of *tangkas*. Originally from Tibet, tangkas are huge fabric banners up to 52 feet long and 36 feet wide, decorated with pictures and symbols. Originally tangkas were made for Buddhist ceremonies, and only a few survived the Communist era. Today several tangkas are being restored, and the art is becoming known once again.[4]

Mongolian Culture Today

Almost three million people live in Mongolia. Life for rural dwellers is much the same as it was centuries ago. Families live in gers on the steppes and travel with their herds as the seasons change. Living in a tiny ger also helps keep Mongolian families close. An extended family might include a husband, wife, their children, grandparents, and even uncles or aunts, all living in one room.

In the cities, life is very different. City dwellers live in apartments, dress in Western-style clothing, and eat Western foods. However, even city dwellers know about Mongolia's traditional rural lifestyle, and many try to maintain ties to this way of life. They may visit relatives or friends on the steppes or vacation there. Some people even leave the city to try life as a nomad. This kind of life is very hard, but it is also full of beauty and freedom—and those are two parts of Mongolian culture that will never die.

Tuvkhun is one of Mongolia's oldest Buddhist monasteries, built in 1654.

Visitors view elaborate tangka tapestries on display in 2004 at Ta'er Monastery in Xining, capital of Qinghai Province, China. A lost art form for generations, tangkas were previously unseen by many people.

What's to Eat?

Most traditional Mongolian food is based on foods available to rural nomads. For this reason traditional meals feature mostly dairy products and meat. Because nomads did not plant crops, there were few fruits or vegetables. Nomads also could not carry ovens with them to bake bread.

During the summer, most traditional Mongolian foods are dairy products, especially cheese and yogurt. A popular Mongolian drink is called *airag*. Airag is made by pouring fresh horse's milk into a skin, along with ingredients that ferment the milk. The milk is stirred regularly and left to ferment until it is very strong.

During the winter, traditional Mongolians rely on meat as the largest part of their diet. Sometimes meat is boiled in a big metal bowl. Other times it is dried or made into a soup called *khorkhog* (see below). Other traditional Mongolian foods include *buuz*, or steamed mutton (sheep) dumplings and *khuushuur*, or fried pancakes made with mutton.[5]

CHAPTER FOUR
Taiwanese Culture

道 Taiwan is a small island off the eastern coast of China. Over the centuries, different cultures have lived on and controlled the island. These varied ethnic groups created an interesting mix of cultures.

History

More than 7,000 years ago, a group most likely from Southeast Asian and Pacific islands settled in Taiwan.[1] Called the Mountain People, this culture became known as the Dapenkeng. At first the Dapenkeng lived in the mountains along the coast, but in time they moved inland and settled on Taiwan's rolling plains.

Because Taiwan is so close to China, Chinese explorers soon found the island. In the 1400s a Chinese explorer named Zheng sailed to Taiwan. Zheng discovered many pirates who had found safety and shelter on the island after raiding Chinese and Japanese communities.

By the late 1500s more of the world knew about Taiwan. Portuguese explorers tried but failed to establish a trading post in northern Taiwan. Then in 1598 the Japanese ruler Tokugawa tried to take over Taiwan. The native tribes worked together to force the Japanese back to a small island settlement called Takasago.

During the 1600s, the Dutch East India Company established a base in Taiwan to buy spices, herbs, silks, and other goods from Japan and China to ship back to Holland and other European countries. The Dutch brought in workers from China to clear the land for farming.

Dutch control of Taiwan did not last long. In 1661 a Chinese naval commander named Zheng Chenggong took control of Taiwan and forced the Dutch off of the island. Zheng, also known as Koxinga, established Chinese rule in Taiwan and is still considered a national hero there today.

Portrait of Tokugawa

Koxinga set up a Chinese style of government in Taiwan and also brought many artists, teachers, and monks to the island. However, he died after just a few months, and his son took over. In 1683 the Qing dynasty in China took control of Taiwan and ruled there for several centuries.

By 1887 Taiwan was a province of China. Then a brief war with Japan forced China to give control of Taiwan to the Japanese. The Taiwanese people, many of whom had Chinese heritage, did not want Japan to govern the island. More than 7,000 people were killed during the first few months of Japanese rule, but the rebellion did not succeed.[2] The Japanese did improve conditions on the island and changed the economy from agriculture to industry.

After Japan lost World War II in 1945, China took back Taiwan. Then in 1949 Mao Zedong's Communist party won control of China. His opposition, Chiang Kai-shek and his Nationalist Party, fled to Taiwan, and they established the Republic of China there.

Today Taiwan has a different government than China and is recognized as a separate country by most of the world—but not by the Chinese government. Despite these difficulties, the two countries are partners economically and socially and share many cultural traditions.

This statue of Zheng Chenggong towers over Gulangyu Island in Xiaman, China.

Taiwan's People

In 2012, 84 percent of Taiwan's citizens were Taiwanese. They are descended from emigrants to Taiwan from China between the 1600s and the 1900s. Ethnic Chinese people made up 14 percent of the population, while native people made up just 2 percent of the population.[3]

Taiwan's native people face many problems. For centuries the Chinese and Japanese governments discriminated against them. Natives are now protected by the government, but they still face many economic problems and struggle to preserve their traditional ways. This is difficult, especially since many have moved away from an agricultural lifestyle and into cities, where they are exposed to Chinese culture. Native languages are also in danger of fading away, although language programs in schools and on television are helping to keep that tradition alive, and an Indigenous Television Network promotes native languages and culture.

As in other cultures, marriage is the base of the family. Taiwanese marriages combine traditional customs with more modern ways. Matchmakers used to introduce men and women to each other and arrange the marriages. Today this is very rare, and most couples meet through family, friends, or at work or school, just as in other countries. A bride often wears three different wedding gowns: a traditional red Chinese gown, a pastel-colored Taiwanese gown, and a white gown like those worn in Western countries.

Religion

People in Taiwan practice several different religions. The most popular are Buddhism, Taoism, folk religions, and Christianity. Many people practice combinations of different religions, such as Taoism and Buddhism.

Taiwan's people have great respect for their ancestors. Most Taiwanese families have shrines in their homes. Here they burn offerings or leave gifts such as food to honor the spirits of the dead and bring good fortune. A special part of folk religion is Ghost Month, when people make offerings to dead ancestors to keep

In May 2014 on Taipei, thousands of Taiwanese Buddhists gather to celebrate both Buddha's birthday and Mother's Day.

their ghosts happy. People also burn paper "ghost money" so ghosts have money to travel to the afterlife.

Sports and the Arts

Taiwan's arts are very similar to China's. Taiwanese people enjoy Chinese opera as well as traditional Chinese arts such as ceramics and painting. Taiwan's classic opera includes four main characters: Chou, a clown; Jing, a troublemaker; Dan, the female lead; and Shen, the male lead.

Martial arts are also an important part of Taiwanese life. Many martial artists appear in action movies, which are hugely popular in Taiwan. People also enjoy more realistic and serious films. Famous director Ang Lee was born in Taiwan. Now a U.S. citizen, he has won Academy Awards for his movies *Crouching Tiger, Hidden Dragon* (Best Foreign Film) and *Life of Pi* (Best Director).

Ang Lee at the 85th Academy Awards.

Taiwanese are very active. Many people ride bikes, jog, dance, or swim. The most popular team sport in Taiwan is baseball. Players from Taiwan have become popular stars in Japan and the United States. Taiwanese athletes who have played in the US Major Leagues include Chien-Ming Wang, Chin-Feng Chen, Chin-lung Hu, and Hong-Chih Kuo.

Taiwanese Culture Today

Taiwan is a very modern nation. Most of its people live in cities and work in factories and businesses. They listen to Western music and enjoy movies, books, and video games from all over the world.

Still, Taiwan's basic culture remains the same. The family is the center of Taiwanese life. Children respect their parents and are encouraged to behave well in public. Elderly relatives and ancestors are also treated with great respect. For a person in Taiwan, nothing is worse than to "lose face," or be embarrassed in public.

Taiwan has seen many changes over its history. This nation is a mix of many different cultures, all of which have combined to create the culture of Taiwan.

Hong-Chih Kuo pitching for the Chinese Taipei national team in the 2013 World Baseball Classic.

Professional Mourners

In Taiwan, you can hire people to mourn at a funeral. The idea of hiring mourners started when young women who lived far away could not return home for a relative's funeral, so families hired a professional mourner as a "replacement daughter." Professional mourners wear white robes and cry loudly during the funeral. Weeping and wailing give the deceased person a big, loud sendoff that will help him or her travel to the afterlife.

Liu Jun-Lin is Taiwan's most famous professional mourner. She learned the job from her mother and grandmother. Liu believes that she helps families when a loved one dies. "This work can really help people release their anger or help them say the things they're afraid to say out loud," she told an interviewer for BBC News in 2013. "For people who are afraid to cry, it helps too because everyone cries together."[4]

A professional mourner of the "Filial Daughters' Band" wears a traditional Taiwanese funeral hood while holding the daughter of a deceased relative at a funeral.

Japanese Culture

道 Japan's culture is a fascinating mix of ancient traditions and modern technology. Japan's culture began more than 10,000 years ago, and ancient traditions continue to affect modern life.

History

Scientists believe that people first arrived in Japan more than 30,000 years ago. At that time, Japan was not an island as it is today. Instead, a land bridge connected Japan to Russia, which enabled hunters to follow their prey into what is now Japan. These people left no written records of their stay in Japan, so we know very little about what their lives were like.

The first ancient Japanese culture we know about is the Jomon culture. The Jomon first arrived in Japan around 10,000 BCE and eventually dominated Japan between 800 and 300 BCE. Nomads at first, the Jomon later settled in communities. Then around 300 BCE the Yayoi people came to power. The Yayoi planted rice and settled in villages near the rice paddies.

After the year 300, Japan established a class system that strictly divided people into groups. Emperors had the most power, followed by skilled craftspeople, farmers, and peasants. Slaves were the lowest class. During this time, Japan began trading with its neighbors, China and Korea. Japanese culture was greatly influenced by China, especially in architecture and design.

Landowners had a lot of power in Japan. As each lord took over land, he also took control of the people who lived and worked there. Residents paid taxes and provided crops and other supplies to their lord in exchange for his protection. The lords hired warriors called samurai to guard their lands and people. In time the samurai became so rich and powerful that they became the highest class in Japanese society. The Age of the Samurai lasted for nearly seven hundred years, from 1185 until 1868.

During the 1860s, European countries were establishing colonies all over the world. Japan avoided becoming a colony, but in 1854 the nation was forced to sign a trade treaty with the United States, which brought even more foreigners into Japan. When Emperor Meiji came to power in 1868, he followed a British-style government. Although the emperor was still the highest ruler, other people became involved in government through a House of Representatives. Meiji also got rid of the samurai class and changed Japan's economy from agricultural to industrial.

By 1895 Japan had a lot of military power. In 1905 Japan defeated Russia to take over Manchuria, which was rich in

Dotaku bronze bell, late Yayoi period, third century CE

Ronin, or masterless samurai, fending off arrows in battle

natural resources. By 1910 Japan had seized Korea, and during World War I, Japan won control of many islands in the Pacific Ocean. In 1937 Japan invaded China.

On December 7, 1941, Japan attacked the US naval base of Pearl Harbor in Hawaii, pulling the United States into World War II. After nearly four years of fierce battle on Japanese-controlled Pacific Ocean islands, the United States dropped two atomic bombs on the Japanese cities of Hiroshima and Nagasaki in August 1945. Japan surrendered and the war ended.

As part of its surrender, Japan gave up control of Korea, Manchuria, and Taiwan, and the US. Army occupied Japan until 1952. Japan was no longer allowed to have an army, and its emperor became a powerless symbol.

Although Japan lost its military power, it gained a lot of economic power, becoming a world leader in manufacturing cars, electronics, and other industrial products. By the 1970s Japan had the world's second-largest economy, after the United States.[1] In the years since, Japan has remained a major economic power.

Japan's People and Culture

In 2013 almost 127 million people lived in Japan.[2] Most Japanese live in large cities such as Tokyo. Space is tight, and apartments and homes are very tiny.

Hiroshima, Japan, in ruins, 1945.

Almost everyone in Japan is ethnically Japanese, although a tiny percentage is Chinese and Korean.[3] Japan does have three native minority groups. The largest is known as the *burakumin*, which means "discriminated communities." The burakumin are considered outcasts because their ancestors worked in jobs that involved killing animals or handling dead animals or people. There are between two and three million burakumin in Japan.[4]

The other minority groups are the Ainu and the Ryukyuans. The Ainu are descended from the ancient Jomon people. Now numbering fewer than 20,000, the Ainu live in a small area on the island of Hokkaido that was set aside for them by the government. The Ryukyuans originally came from the Ryukyu Islands, which are southwest of Japan. Today most Ryukyuans live on the island of Okinawa.

Japanese families are very traditional. Most fathers work while mothers are responsible for running the household. A child's job is to go to school. Japanese schools are very strict and demanding. If a student gets into a good high school, he or she can go on to attend a top college and get a good job.

Japan's indigenous Ainu people demonstrate a traditional folk dance at Nibutani Ainu Museum on Hokkaido in northern Japan.

Religion

Almost all Japanese follow a religion called Shinto, or "the way of the gods." Shinto believes that gods are everywhere, and they have the power to make people's lives better or worse. There are millions of Shinto spirits, or *kami*, connected to natural objects such as trees or the sun. Prayers and offerings are made to the kami to bring good fortune. Many Japanese have altars in their homes, where they make offerings such as rice cakes and holy water to Shinto gods.

Buddhism is also a major faith in Japan, and many people follow both Shinto and Buddhism. It is common for people to follow Shinto traditions when someone is born or marries but to follow Buddhist practices when a person dies.

Literature and Art

Beauty is very important in Japanese culture, and it is often expressed in the arts. One of the best known parts of Japanese culture is its traditional theater, which includes three types of plays. Noh theater are dramas based on themes from history or classic literature. Actors wear masks and use deliberate movements and dances to tell their stories. Kabuki theater, on the other hand, is filled with action and drama. Performers wear elaborate makeup and wigs, with colors that indicate different emotions such as anger, fear, and sorrow. Finally, Bunraku is puppet theater. Bunraku puppets are very elaborate and can be more than three feet tall.

Art is also very important to the Japanese. One of the most popular arts is paper-folding, or origami. Skilled origami artists can create all sorts of animals and other figures out of folded paper. Another paper art is *kirie*, or paper cutting. A kirie artist cuts pieces out of a sheet of paper to create an image or scene.

Japanese poetry dates back to the eighth century, when 4,500 poems were published in a book called *Manyoshu (The Collection of Ten Thousand Leaves)*. These poems included haiku, which is a

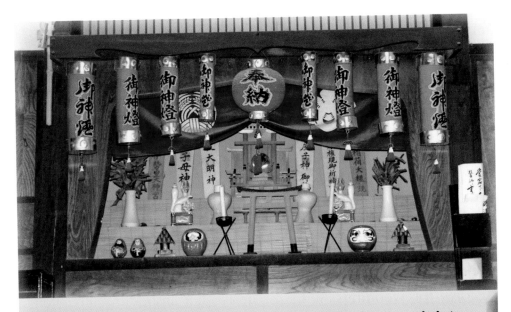

Kamidana ("god-shelf" in Japanese) are miniature household altars to enshrine a Shinto kami, or spirit/force. They are most commonly found in Japan, the home of kami worship.

Bunraku (puppet play) developed over twelve centuries as a popular Japanese entertainment.

seventeen-syllable, three-line poem, and tanka, which are thirty-one-syllable, five-line poems. Both types of poetry focus on plants, animals, and nature.

The world's oldest novel, *The Tale of Genji*, was written in Japan more than one thousand years ago. The novel was set in the emperor's court. Later works featured folktales, romances, and action tales filled with samurai warriors.

Today the most popular style of Japanese literature is manga, graphic novels that combine bright illustrations with fanciful stories. Manga is popular all over the world.

Japanese Culture Today

Although Japan is a modern country whose people enjoy Western music, foods, and clothes, traditional Japanese culture is alive and well. Japanese people still eat traditional foods and follow ancient customs for weddings, funerals, and other important life events. They gather at religious shrines to celebrate holidays and honor their gods. Japanese culture also lives on in the nation's art, literature, theater, and movies, many of which feature ancient stories and themes. Japan may be a nation filled with modern technology, but it is still a very traditional land.

A Japanese Tea Ceremony

In Japan, drinking tea is not just a way to enjoy a beverage but an elaborate ceremony that goes back more than one thousand years. Tea ceremonies are usually held in tea houses or special rooms that are simply but beautifully decorated. A traditional Japanese tea ceremony follows a specific ritual to serve a kind of powdered green tea called *matcha*, along with sweet snacks, in a way that brings peace and harmony to everyone involved. The person serving the tea follows precise movements and customs while preparing and serving the tea. The purpose of the ceremony is to focus on the senses and enjoy the beauty of the present moment. A formal tea ceremony can last up to four hours, and masters of the art often spend many years learning everything they can to create a perfect ceremony.

Most people no longer have tea rooms in their homes or the time to indulge in an hours-long ceremony. However, millions of people study "The Way of the Tea" and go to weekly classes to learn about this traditional art and share it with others.[5]

Dressed in a traditional costume, a kneeling woman scoops water from a bowl during a Japanese tea ceremony.

CHAPTER SIX
South Korean and North Korean Culture

道 For most of history, South Korea and North Korea were one country: Korea. However, after World War II ended in 1945, Korea faced another war and separation into two very different countries. Despite their differences today, North Korea and South Korea share the same history and many of the same cultural traditions.

History

Modern Koreans trace their ancestry to settlers who moved from central Asia onto the Korean Peninsula around 3000 BCE. Nomads at first, these settlers later became farmers and established villages. In time they founded the Ancient Joseon Kingdom in what is now part of China and North Korea. Korean legend explains that Korea was created when Hwanung, the son of the ruler of heaven, transformed a bear into a woman and married her. Together they had a child named Tangun, who became the founder of the first Korean kingdom.

In 109 BCE the emperor of China invaded Ancient Joseon but eventually lost control of the area. Three kingdoms then arose: the Silla, the Baekje, and the Goguryeo. By 668 CE the Silla had conquered the other two kingdoms and controlled Korea for the next 250 years. Silla's people lived under a strict class system. A person's rank determined what kind of clothes they wore, where they lived, and how many goods they could own. Peasant farmers owned their land, although they had to pay taxes and work for the government.

The Silla dynasty ruled Korea until the early 900s. The last Silla king married the daughter of a general named Wang Kon. Wang Kon established a new dynasty, called Goryeo, in 918. The name "Korea" comes from the word Goryeo. Goryeo kings stressed knowledge and the arts and did away with some of the strict class system. During this time, Koreans developed beautiful pottery and woodblock printing. In 1234 they used the world's first movable metal type.[1]

The Mongols invaded Korea in 1231 and destroyed Goryeo culture. Many people lost their land and their freedom. The Mongols were pushed out of Korea more than one hundred years later. General Yi Song-gye seized power and became king in 1392. He established the Joseon dynasty, which ruled Korea for 600 years. During this time, Korea faced many attacks and invasions from Manchuria and Japan. In defense, Korea's rulers cut

Covered ewer, first half of the twelfth century, of stoneware with underglaze slip decoration and celadon glaze. Celadon ceramics of the Goryeo dynasty (918–1392) are among the most celebrated works of Korean art.

47

off contact with all countries except for China during the 1640s. Korea became known as the Hermit Kingdom.

Japan was too powerful a nation to stay out of Korea forever. In 1876 Japan forced the Joseon dynasty to open Korea's ports to Japanese trade. Soon afterward merchants, missionaries, and government representatives from the United States and many European countries came to Korea. By the end of the 1800s, the Joseon dynasty had lost much of its power.

In 1895 Japan waged a war with China that resulted in Korea being recognized as an independent country. Fifteen years later Korea became a colony of Japan. Many Koreans fought against Japanese control. In 1919 the Japanese killed about 7,500 Koreans protesting Japanese rule. After that, many Koreans fled to the Soviet Union. Another group fled to Shanghai, China, where they formed the Provisional Government of the Republic of Korea, ruled in exile by a man named Syngman Rhee.

After its defeat in World War II, Japan gave up control of Korea, which was divided into two areas. The Soviet Union took control of the northern part of Korea while the United States controlled the south. The Soviet Union soon closed the border and refused to reunite the countries under one government. In July 1948 Syngman Rhee was elected president of South Korea. One month later, Kim Il-sung was appointed as premier, or leader, of the Communist government in North Korea.

In 1950 Kim Il-sung invaded South Korea in an attempt to reunite the countries under Communist control. The United States and China got involved, and the war escalated. In 1953 a ceasefire was finally called. The war never officially ended, however, and the two countries remain divided.

After the Korean War, North Korea became a true "hermit kingdom." Kim Il-sung demanded total loyalty from his people, and he did not want them to trust any other nations. Schools taught children that Japan and the United States were enemies who would attack North Korea at any moment. The government also released a lot of propaganda to convince people that other nations were against North Korea. To prevent anyone from hearing a different opinion, Kim cut off all contact with the rest of the world. Anyone who spoke against Kim could be sent to prison or even killed.

By the time Kim Il-sung died in 1994, North Korea was in dire economic shape. The Soviet Union's Communist government had collapsed in the early 1990s, cutting off the foreign aid that had kept North Korea going. A terrible famine followed, and millions of North Koreans starved to death. This tragedy changed little in the government. Kim Il-sung's son, Kim Jong-il, took control and kept the country even more isolated from the rest of the world. After Jong-il's death in 2010, his son Kim Jong-un took over and has continued North Korea's isolationist and repressive government.

Meanwhile, South Korea went through a series of governments, mostly under harsh military rule. South Koreans lost many personal freedoms, but their economy shifted from agricultural to industrial, and the nation became a strong manufacturing center. In October 1987 a democratic constitution was finally approved. South Koreans

This undated picture released from North Korea's official Korean Central News Agency (KCNA) on June 7, 2014, shows North Korean leader Kim Jong-Un (second from left) visiting the Mangyongdae Revolutionary School in Pyongyang.

were allowed to hold free elections, and the country gradually became more democratic.

Korea's People and Families

Most South Koreans live in cities like the capital, Seoul. Korean cities are very modern and very crowded. North Korea is bigger than South Korea, but it has a much smaller population. Most North Koreans live in cities or in the western part of the country. The largest city in North Korea is the capital, Pyongyang.

In North Korea loyalty to the government is of primary importance. People who are loyal to the government are part of the highest social class. They receive the best jobs, housing, and food. People who are neutral about the government are monitored by authorities, although for the most part they are allowed to live their lives in peace. However, the neutral class can't have good jobs or as many consumer goods as people in the loyal class. People who are hostile to the government are the lowest social class and face constant monitoring and punishment for even small

Tourists and shoppers jam the streets of Insadong in Seoul, South Korea. Insadong is a popular tourist destination in Seoul that offers a variety of traditional crafts and goods, along with the usual souvenirs.

offenses. One woman fled the country because she had been caught listening to pop music on a South Korean radio station and faced time in a labor camp as punishment.[2]

Although daily life in South Korea and North Korea is very different, people still have many of the same beliefs and traditions. In both countries one's position in the family is very important. Korean names generally have three parts. The family name comes first. The second name is a generation name, which is shared by all family members in that generation. The last name is a given name (what Westerners call a "first name"). Women are usually called by their relationship to their husband or children. A woman may be called "Mr. Kim's wife" or "Euna's mother." Marriage is extremely important in Korean culture, and a person who doesn't have a partner or children is not considered a true adult.

Religion

Buddhism was once the most important religion in Korea. It was introduced to Korea by the Chinese around 370. Later, Koreans followed the teachings of a Chinese scholar named Confucius. Confucius instructed people to be kind, honest, and loving, to respect their elders and their rulers, and to live a good life. These beliefs still shape the lives of North and South Koreans today.

A Buddhist temple in the Pukhan mountains in South Korea.

Today South Koreans follow many different religions, although Buddhism and Confucianism are the most popular. Many Koreans also call themselves Christian, following a religion introduced by missionaries hundreds of years ago. Another popular Korean religion is Cheondogyo (also spelled Ch'ŏndogyo), which was created in Korea as a reaction to Western teachings. Almost half of South Koreans say they follow some religion, and many accept the beliefs of more than one faith.[3]

Things are very different in North Korea. Although the country's constitution says there is freedom of religion, the Communist government thinks that any religious beliefs prevent a person from being loyal to the state. Since the 1950s, North Korea's government has banned religious activities and persecuted people for their faith. For this reason very few North Koreans practice any type of religion.

Music and Art

Korea has a rich cultural and artistic background. For centuries Korean artists have worked with wood, ceramics, and cloth to create beautiful works of art. Scenes from nature are especially popular as are bright colors and geometric patterns.

Korea is also famous for its paper crafts. Artists glue many layers of paper together to make a strong surface, then paint colorful designs on the paper and varnish it to make it shiny. Kites, lanterns, and fans are some of the most popular paper creations.

South Koreans enjoy traditional music and art, but they also take part in more modern pursuits. A type of music called K-pop is extremely popular in Asian countries and has spread to Western countries as well.

In North Korea, music, art, and literature are tightly controlled by the government. Artists are instructed to paint images of the country's leaders that show them smiling and often bathed in bright light. North Korean writers are also expected to write stories that show the Kim dynasty in a positive light and leaders of other nations as villains. Along with glorifying North Korea's leaders, these stories are also meant to inspire people to work hard and completely support the Kim dynasty. Similarly, North Korean operas glorify the state and its leaders and depict their amazing accomplishments.

Korean Culture Today

South Korea and North Korea are very different countries. South Korea is modern and energetic, filled with high-tech devices and busy people. North Koreans have a more difficult life because of government policies and shortages of food and other necessities. North Korea lacks most modern technology common in South Korea and other parts of the world.

But many things remain the same in both countries. Citizens in both nations value family and enjoy spending time with relatives and friends. People in both cultures enjoy traditional holidays and customs, value order, and do their best to be good citizens. Though North and South Korea have very different economies, governments, and lifestyles, their people come from the same traditions and still practice many of them today.

Korean artists create amazing things with paper. The traditional art of hanji includes pictures, dolls, and other handicrafts made from paper handmade from mulberry bark.

Korean Foods

Korean foods are known for variety and hot spices. Sticky white rice is eaten at every meal, but many other foods go with it. Kimchi—spicy pickled cabbage—is a favorite food in both North and South Korea. Another popular Korean dish is bulgogi, also called Korean barbecue, which contains strips of beef and vegetables cooked over a grill.

Korean meals are served on a low table with people sitting on the floor. Each person has his or her own bowl of rice and a bowl of soup. Side dishes such as vegetables, meat, fish, kimchi, and sauces are arranged in the middle of the table for everyone to share. Diners eat with chopsticks and dip the food into sauces to add flavor.

Kimchi

Bulgogi

Map of East Asia

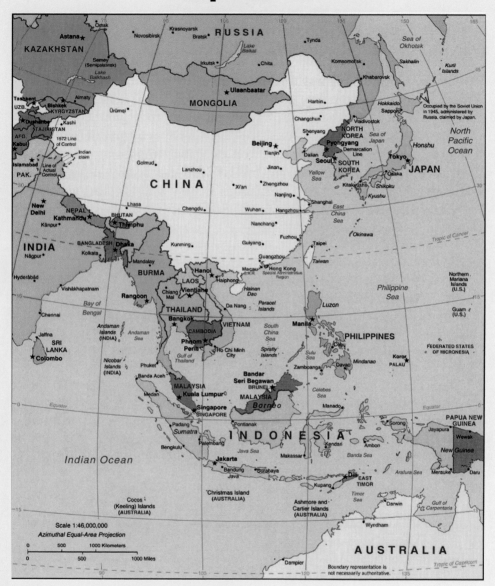

Experiencing East Asian Culture in the United States

The countries of East Asia may be far away from your home, but there are many ways to explore East Asian culture here in the United States. Many major cities have museums dedicated to Asian art, history, and culture. If you can, visit one of these museums. If that isn't possible, have fun exploring their Websites to see photographs and videos of what these museums have to offer.

ASIAN MUSEUMS IN THE UNITED STATES

Asian Art Museum, San Francisco, California
http://www.asianart.org

China Institute in America, New York, New York
http://www.chinainstitute.org

Chinese American Museum, Los Angeles, California
http://www.camla.org

The Chinese-American Museum of Chicago, Chicago, Illinois
http://www.ccamuseum.org

Chinese Culture Center of San Francisco, San Francisco, California
http://www.c-c-c.org

Chinese Historical Society of America, San Francisco, California
http://www.chsa.org

The Chinese Workers Museum, Carson City, Nevada
http://www.chineseworkersmuseum.org

Japanese American National Museum, Los Angeles, California
http://www.janm.org

Korean American Museum, Los Angeles, California
http://www.kamuseum.org

Martial Arts History Museum, Los Angeles, California
      http://www.mamuseum.com
Morikami Museum and Japanese Gardens, Delray Beach, Florida
      http://www.morikami.org
Museum of the Chinese in America, New York, New York
      http://www.mocanyc.org
Pacific Asia Museum, Pasadena, California
      http://www.pacificasiamuseum.org
Portland Chinese Classical Garden, Portland, Oregon
      http://www.portlandchinesegarden.org
San Diego Chinese Historical Museum, San Diego, California
      http://www.sdchm.org
Seattle Asian Art Museum, Seattle, Washington
      http://www.seattleartmuseum.org
Texas State Museum of Asian Cultures, Corpus Christi, Texas
      http://www.asianculturesmuseum.org
The Wing Luke Asian Museum, Seattle, Washington
      http://www.wingluke.org

In addition, many major US cities, especially those on the West Coast, have Chinatowns, Japantowns, or other ethnic neighborhoods. These neighborhoods are filled with traditional Asian stores and restaurants and are great places to get a real taste of Asian culture.

Asian restaurants are also a wonderful place to experience ethnic food and learn about traditional customs. Check out review sites on the Internet to find an Asian restaurant near you, and then give your taste buds a special treat!

TIMELINE

BCE

8000–300	The Jomon culture arises in Japan.
4000–3000	The Dapenkeng culture arises in Taiwan.
About 2000	The first Chinese dynasty, the Xia, comes to power.
300s	The Choson culture emerges in Korea.

CE

668	Korea is brought together under the rule of the Silla.
759	*Manyoshu, A Collection of Ten Thousand Leaves* is published in Japan.
935	The Goryeo dynasty comes to power in Korea.
1050	The samurai rise to power in Japan.
1215	Genghis Khan's army captures Beijing, the capital of China.
1260	Khublai Khan becomes leader of Mongolia.
1392	The Choson dynasty takes control of Korea.
1624	The Dutch establish settlements in Taiwan.
1641	Japan's emperor bans foreigners from the country.
1661	Zheng Chenggong (Koxinga) takes control of Taiwan from the Dutch.
1683	China's Qing rulers take over Taiwan.
1854	The United States forces Japan to allow trade with foreigners.
1877	The samurai are defeated in the Satsuma Rebellion.
1895	Japan wins control of Taiwan after a war with China.
1905	Japan wins control of Korea after a war with Russia.
1910	Korea becomes a Japanese colony.
1911	Mongolia declares its independence.
1912	The Republic of China is founded.
1919	More than seven thousand Koreans are killed protesting against Japanese government.
1920s–1930s	The Communist government destroys the Buddhist religion in Mongolia.
1931	Japan invades Manchuria.
1937	Japan declares war on China.
1941	Japan bombs Pearl Harbor, causing the United States to enter World War II.
1945	Japan surrenders after the US drops two atomic bombs on the country, ending World War II; Taiwan is returned to China at the end of World War II; Korea is divided into two countries.
1948	North Korea and South Korea establish separate governments.
1949	Communist leader Mao Zedong establishes the People's Republic of China; Chaing Kai-shek and his Nationalist followers flee to Taiwan.
1950–1953	North and South Korea fight the Korean War.
1966	China's Cultural Revolution begins.
1978	Mao Zedong dies; Deng Xiaoping comes to power.
1987	South Korea adopts a democratic constitution.
1990	Communism ends in Mongolia.
2014	More than three hundred people die in a ferry disaster in South Korea, leading to the resignation of the prime minister.

CHAPTER NOTES

Chapter 1. Gung Hay Fat Choy!

1. Grace Huang, "11 Things to Know About Lunar New Year." http://www.cnn.com/2014/01/27/travel/11-things-/ny-
2. Chinese New Year, "Chinese New Year Traditions," http://www.chinesenewyears.info/
3. Ibid.
4. Ibid.
5. Whats-Your-Sign.com, "Chinese Zodiac Signs and Meanings," http://www.whats-your-sign.com/Chinese-zodiac-signs.html

Chapter 2. Chinese Culture

1. *China Culture*, "Han Ethnic Group," http://www1.chinaculture.org/library/2008-02/05/content_23849.htm
2. Personal observation of the author.
3. *The Buddhist Centre: Buddhism for Today*, "Who Was the Buddha?" https://thebuddhistcentre.com/text/who-was-buddha
4. *Travel China Guide*, "Chinese Opera," http://www.travelchinaguide.com/intro/arts/chinese-opera.htm
5. Personal observation of the author.
6. Ping Zhou, "Tourism Development in China," http://geography.about.com/od/chinamaps/a/Tourism-Development-In-China.htm
7. *Academic Dictionaries and Encyclopedias:Encyclopedia of Contemporary Chinese Culture*, "Gender Roles," http://contemporary_chinese_culture.academic.ru/279/gender_roles

Chapter 3. Mongolian Culture

1. Allison Lassieur, *Mongolia* (Enchantment of the World Series. New York: Children's Press, 2007), p. 81.
2. Ibid, p. 81.
3. Discover Mongolia, http://www.discovermongolia.mn/blog-news/mongolian-food.php
4. Lassieur, p. 115.
5. Discover Mongolia, http://www.discovermongolia.mn/blog-news/mongolian-food.php

Chapter 4. Taiwanese Culture

1. Dr. Sim Kiantek, *The True History of Taiwan*, http://www.taiwannation.com.tw/english.htm
2. Barbara A. Somervill, *Taiwan*, Enchantment of the World Series (New York: Children's Press, 2014), p. 52.
3. "Taiwan Demographics Profile 2013," http://www.indexmundi.com/taiwan/demographics_profile.html
4. Allie Jaynes, "Taiwan's Most Famous Professional Mourner," http://www.bbc.com/news/magazine-21479399

Chapter 5. Japanese Culture

1. Barbara A. Somervill, *Japan*, Enchantment of the World Series (New York: Children's Press, 2012), p. 57.
2. "Japan Population 2013," http://www.worldpopulationstatistics.com/japan-population-2013/
3. Ibid., p. 85.

CHAPTER NOTES

4. The Burakumin: Japan's Invisible Race," http://www.tofugu.com/2011/ 11/18/the-burakumin-japans- invisible-race/

5. "Japan Fact Sheet: Tea Ceremony: The Way of Tea," http://web-japan.org/factsheet/en/ pdf/28TeaCeremony.pdf

Chapter 6. South Korean and North Korean Culture

1. "Movable Type," www.artsmia.org/art-of-asia/history/ korea-koryo-dynasty.cfm

2. Liz Sonneborn, *North Korea*, Enchantment of the World Series (New York: Children's Press, 2014), p. 86.

3. Patricia J. Kummer, *South Korea*, Enchantment of the World Series (New York: Children's Press, 2008), p. 88.

FURTHER READING

Books

Catel, Patrick. *China*. Chicago: Heinemann Library, 2012.

Kummer, Patricia J. *South Korea*. Enchantment of the World Series. New York: Children's Press, 2008.

Lassieur, Allison. *Mongolia*. Enchantment of the World Series. New York: Children's Press, 2007.

Levin, Judith. *Japanese Mythology*. New York: Rosen Central, 2007.

Mara, Wil. *People's Republic of China*. Enchantment of the World Series. New York: Children's Press, 2012.

Mattern, Joanne. *Recipe and Craft Guide to China*. Hockessin, DE: Mitchell Lane Publishers, 2011.

Mofford, Juliet Haines. *Recipe and Craft Guide to Japan*. Hockessin, DE: Mitchell Lane Publishers, 2010.

Senker, Cath. *North Korea and South Korea*. New York: Rosen, 2013.

Somervill, Barbara A. *Japan*. Enchantment of the World Series. New York: Children's Press, 2012.

Somervill, Barbara A. *Taiwan*. Enchantment of the World Series. New York: Children's Press, 2014.

Sonneborn, Liz. *North Korea*. Enchantment of the World Series. New York: Children's Press, 2014.

Works Consulted

Mah, Adeline Yen. *China: Land of Dragons and Emperors*. New York: Delacorte Press, 2009.

Uschan, Michael V. *China Since World War II*. Detroit: Lucent Books, 2009.

On the Internet

AJ Panda: "Chinese Museums in the United States" http://www.ajpanda.com/Articles.asp?ID=190

FURTHER READING

CIA: *The World Factbook*, "East & Southeast Asia: China"
  https://www.cia.gov/library/publications/the-world-factbook/geos/ch.html
National Geographic: "China Facts"
  http://travel.nationalgeographic.com/travel/countries/china-facts/
Discover Mongolia: "Mongolia Food"
  http://www.discovermongolia.mn/blog-news/mongolian-food.php
Enchanted Learning: *All about China*
  http://www.enchantedlearning.com/asia/china/
World Population Statistics: Countries, "Japan Population 2013"
  http://www.worldpopulationstatistics.com/japan-population-2013/
Japanese Tea Ceremony: *The Japanese Tea Ceremony*
  http://japanese-tea-ceremony.net/
Jaynes, Allie. "Taiwan's Most Famous Professional Mourner"
  http://www.bbc.com/news/magazine-21479399
Kiantek, Dr. Sim. *The True History of Taiwan*
  http://www.taiwannation.com.tw/english.htm
Kids Web Japan: *Virtual Culture*
  http://web-japan.org/kidsweb/virtual/
National Geographic Kids: *Countries*, "Find People & Places: China, Facts and Photos"
  http://kids.nationalgeographic.com/kids/places/find/china/
Time for Kids: *Around the World*, "China"
  http://www.timeforkids.com/destination/china
Travel China Guide: *Chinese Culture*, "Chinese Opera"
  http://www.travelchinaguide.com/intro/arts/chinese-opera.htm
Travel China Guide: *Chinese Culture*, "Chinese Zodiac: 12 Animal Signs"
  http://www.travelchinaguide.com/intro/social_customs/zodiac/
Ministry of Education, Republic of China: "People and Culture of Taiwan"
  http://english.moe.gov.tw/ct.asp?xItem=586&ctNode=3008&mp=2
Mongolia Today
  http://www.mongoliatoday.com
Mongolian Ways
  http://www.mongolian-ways.com
Princeton: "Movable Type"
  www.artsmia.org/art-of-asia/history/korea-koryo-dynasty.cfm
Tofugu: "The Burakumin: Japan's Invisible Race"
  http://www.tofugu.com/2011/11/18/the-burakumin-japans-invisible-race/
Travel China Guide: *Chinese Culture*, "Chinese Opera"
  http://www.travelchinaguide.com/intro/arts/chinese-opera.htm
Web Japan: "Japan Fact Sheet: Tea Ceremony; The Way of Tea"
  http://web-japan.org/factsheet/en/pdf/28TeaCeremony.pdf

GLOSSARY

agriculture (AG-ruh-kuhl-chur)—Farming.

ancestors (AN-sess-turz)—Members of a family who lived a long time ago.

ancient (AYN-shunt)—Very old.

colonies (KOL-uh-neez)—Territory that is controlled by another country.

Communist (KOM-yoo-nuhst)—A person who supports Communism, a political system in which the entire community owns all property equally.

democratic (dem-uh-KRAT-ik)—When all people have equal rites.

discriminated (diss-KRIM-uh-nayt-ed)—Treated unfairly.

dynasties (DYE-nuh-steez)—Lines of rulers belonging to the same family.

emperors (EM-per-urs)—Male rulers of an empire.

ethnic (ETH-nik)—Relating to a group that shares a common culture or heritage.

famine (FAM-uhn)—A serious lack of food.

ferment (fur-MENT)—A chemical change in a drink that turns sugar into alcohol.

indigenous (in-DIDG-uh-nuss)—Native.

industry (IN-duh-stree)—Manufacturing and other businesses.

martial arts (MAR-shuhl ARTS)—A style of fighting that comes from East Asia.

media (MEE-dee-uh)—Ways of getting information to people, such as television, radio, and the Internet.

meditation (med-uh-TAY-shuhn)—The act of relaxing the mind and thinking very deeply about something.

missionaries (MISH-uh-ner-eez)—People sent by a church or religious group to teach that religion to others.

monasteries (MON-uh-ster-eez)—Buildings where monks live and work.

monks (MUNKZ)—Men who live in a religious community.

mourn (MORN)—To feel very sad because someone has died.

myths (MITHS)—Stories that express the beliefs of a group of people or give reasons for things that happen in nature.

natives (NAY-tivs)—People born in a particular place.

naval (NAY-vuhl)—Having to do with a navy or fleet of ships.

nomads (NOH-madz)—People who wander instead of living in one place.

peasants (PEZ-uhntz)—People who work on small farms.

propaganda (prop-uh-GAN-duh)—Information that is spread to influence the way people think.

prosperity (pross-PARE-uh-tee)—Success, especially financial success.

province (PROV-uhnss)—A region of some countries.

rural (RUR-uhl)—Having to do with life in the country.

shrines (SHRINEZ)—Holy places.

traditions (truh-DISH-uhnz)—Customs, ideas, and beliefs that are handed down from one generation to the next.

treaty (TREE-tee)—A formal agreement between two or more countries.

urban (UR-buhn)—Having to do with life in the city.

Western (WEST-uhrn)—relating to countries in the Western part of the world, such as the United States and countries in Europe.

INDEX

About the Author

Joanne Mattern is the author of many books for children on a variety of subjects, including history, biography, and nature. She has written many biographies for Mitchell Lane, as well as several books about China's food and culture. Joanne and her husband traveled to China to adopt their children and found those journeys to be amazing experiences! Joanne lives in New York State with her husband, children, and several pets.